WHEN I GROW UP
I'LL BE A VETERINARIAN

BY CONNIE COLWELL MILLER   ILLUSTRATED BY SILVIA BARONCELLI

AMICUS ILLUSTRATED • RIVERSTREAM

AMICUS ILLUSTRATED is published by Amicus
P.O. Box 1329, Mankato, MN 56002
www.amicuspublishing.us

Paperback edition printed by RiverStream Publishing in arrangement with Amicus.
ISBN 978-1-62243-365-0 (paperback)

LIBRARY OF CONGRESS CATALOGING-IN-PUBLICATION DATA
Miller, Connie Colwell, 1976– author.
I'll be a veterinarian / by Connie Colwell Miller.
    pages cm. — (When I grow up . . .)
Other title: When I grow up I'll be a veterinarian
Audience: K to grade 3.
Summary: "A young boy pretends to be a veterinarian while playing with a friend after
school, showing what it's like to be a professional veterinarian"— Provided by publisher.
ISBN 978-1-60753-764-9 (library binding) — ISBN 978-1-60753-863-9 (ebook)
1. Veterinarians—Juvenile literature. 2. Veterinary medicine—Juvenile literature. I.
Baroncelli, Silvia, illustrator. II. Title. III. Title: I will be a veterinarian. IV. Title: When
I grow up I'll be a veterinarian.
SF612.M55 2016
636.089—dc23   2015029350

EDITOR   Rebecca Glaser
DESIGNER   Kathleen Petelinsek

Printed in the United States of America at
Corporate Graphics in North Mankato, Minnesota.

HC 10 9 8 7 6 5 4 3 2 1
PB 10 9 8 7 6 5 4 3 2 1

ABOUT THE AUTHOR
Connie Colwell Miller is a writer, reader, and teacher who lives in Mankato,
Minnesota. When she was little she always knew she would work with two things:
kids and books. Today, her dream has come true. She has written over 80 books
for kids, and she lives with four wonderful, creative children of her own.

ABOUT THE ILLUSTRATOR
Silvia Baroncelli has loved to draw since she was a child. She collaborates regularly
with publishers in drawing and graphic design from her home in Prato, Italy.
Her best collaborators are her four nephews, daughters Ginevra and Irene, and
organized husband Tommaso. Find out more about her at silviabaroncelli.it

… I am Dr. Thomas, a veterinarian! I am a doctor for pets. My first patient is a cat named Tab. She needs her yearly checkup. I look in her ears and eyes. I check her teeth. I listen to her heart and lungs with a stethoscope.

Now, Tab needs a shot. This vaccination will help prevent Tab from getting diseases in the future. Great news! Tab is healthy and ready to go home!

My next patient is a hamster named Pinky. Pinky's owner has never owned a hamster before. First, I make sure Pinky is healthy. Then, I teach his owner how to care for Pinky.

HAMSTER CARE

My next patient is a dog named Rufus. Rufus hurt his leg chasing squirrels. Rufus's owner is worried. I tell the owner that Rufus is in good hands—mine!

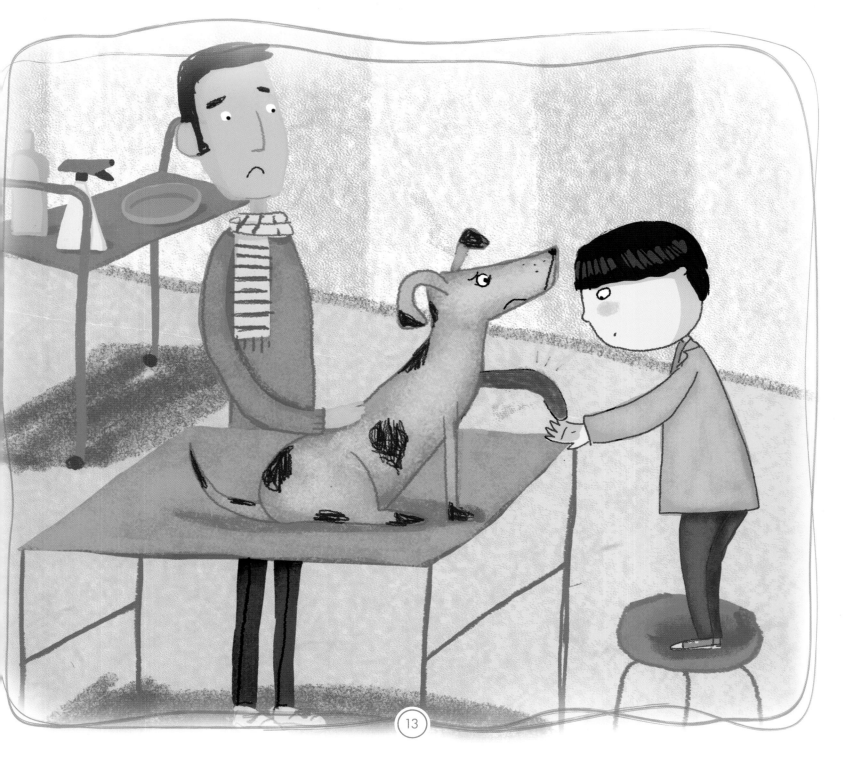

I gently examine Rufus's leg. It's broken. X-rays show where the break is. Rufus will need a cast. But he will be okay.

I call in a vet tech. She's my assistant, and she helps me set Rufus's leg. We also give Rufus's owner some medicine to help with the dog's pain.

Rufus will need to wear his cast until his bone heals. It won't be easy. But Rufus—and his owner—are feeling much better when they leave.

I am done at the office for today. But my work is not over. I am "on call" tonight. This means that if a pet needs emergency care, I will be asked to help.

When I grow up, I'll be a real veterinarian. I will help all kinds of animals. As you can see, Rufus (I mean, Julia!) feels great! But for now, mom says it's time for supper.

WORDS VETS SHOULD KNOW

disease—A type of illness, usually serious.

examine—To check over something very carefully.

patient—A person or animal that needs health care.

stethoscope—A tool with a round disk and tubes that go to a person's ears, used to listen to sounds made by the heart and lungs.

vaccination—A shot of medicine that helps prevent illness.

vet tech—A trained assistant for a veterinarian.

x-ray—A special picture that allows vets to see animals' bones.

PRACTICE BEING A VET MAKE YOUR OWN DOG TREATS

 Vets help make sure animals get healthy food. Ask an adult to help you make these yummy dog treats!

WHAT YOU NEED

2 ¼ cups (340 mL) whole wheat flour
¼ cup (65 mL) applesauce
1 egg
½ cup (125 mL) hot water
¼ cup (65 mL) oil

1 chicken bouillon cube
1 tablespoon (15 mL) honey
1 tablespoon (15 mL) molasses
1 cup (250 mL) carob chips

WHAT YOU DO

1. Wash your hands. Knead all the ingredients except the carob chips together on a lightly floured surface until a dough forms.
2. Press dough flat. Use cookie cutters to cut dough into shapes for a dog.
3. Bake the treats at 300°F (150°C) for 30 minutes. Let them cool.
4. Put the carob chips in a microwaveable bowl. Melt them in the microwave.
5. Dip the treats in the melted carob chips.
6. Refrigerate treats. Serve them to your dog as a reward for good behavior or learning a new trick.